Day
Night
Vs
Ying Vs Yang
N
W   E
S
Straight
Curvy
Black
Vs
White
Make
Good
Choices
Open
Notes
Vs
Closed
Candy
Vs
Fruit
Down
Up
High
Low
In
Out
AF479620
Written and illustrated by Jill Smart

MAKE GOOD CHOICES

JILL SMART

ReadersMagnet, LLC

Dedicated to:
my family,
~Don—Husband
~Emily—Daughter
~Hannah—Daughter
~Harry—Dad
~Gerry—Mom
And all of my former students!

"Make Good Choices,"
my mom always
says.

Nucleic Acids
RNA
ribonucleic acid
DNA
deoxyribonucleic acid
Make Good Choices!
BIOLOGY
Chargaff's Rules
DNA   C → G
      A → T
RNA   T = U
      A → U

She learned this from
her father who has been
known to wear a fez.

You can flock with
the turkeys,

Or soar with the
eagles,

It is totally

up to

you!

She often reminds
me of the
right thing
to do!

Eat your vegetables!
They are good for you!

Always tell
the
truth!

I, _______,
promise to
tell the truth,
the whole truth,
and nothing but
the truth
so help me,
God

And remember
to be
kind!

This will put you
in the
right frame of
mind!

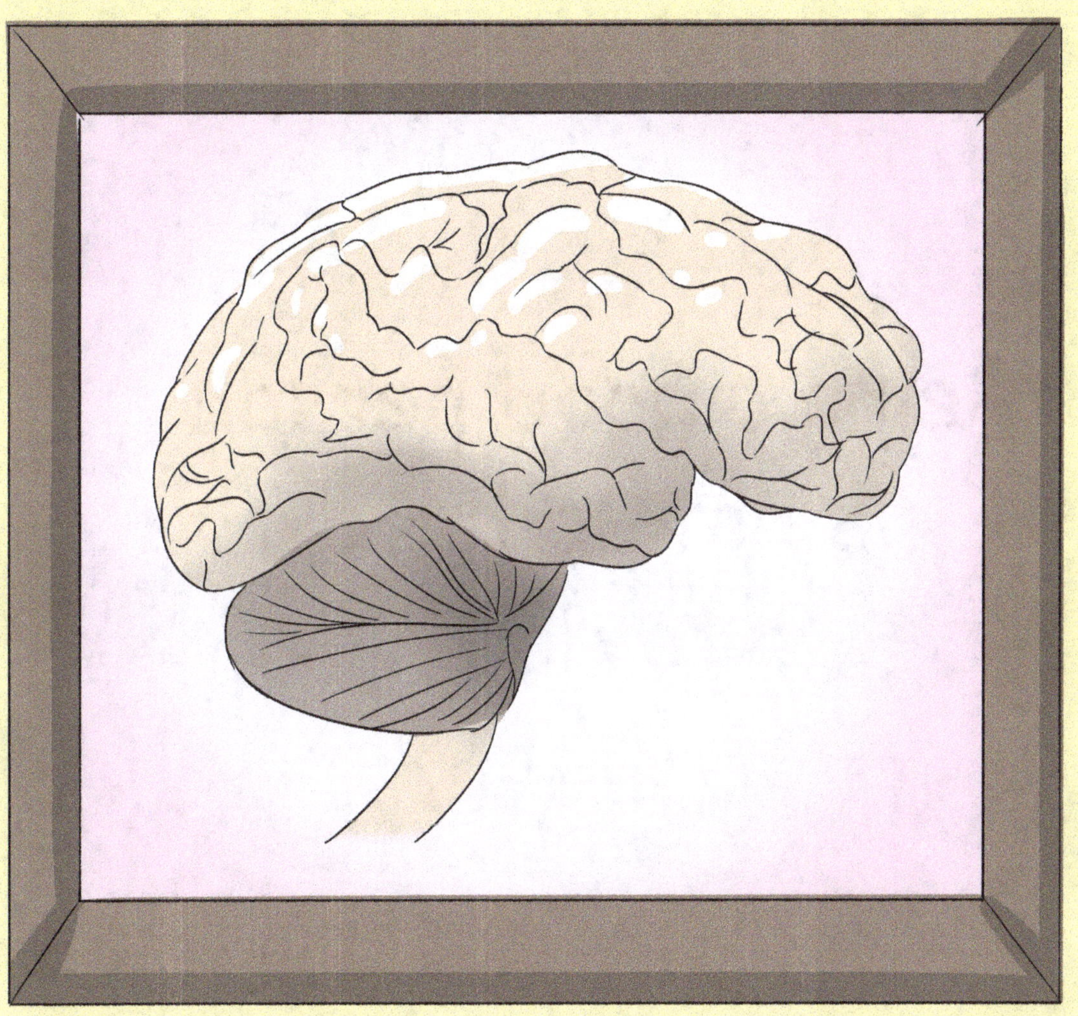

Being a good person
is not so hard
to do,

Just be mindful of
what choice is
best for
you!

Left or Right?
Chocolate
or
vanilla?
Carrots
or
Chips?
Oh,
my!
Which way
should
I go?
Up
or
Down
Night
or
Day?